Praise for *She Tastes Like Possibility*

"Nicole Perriella-Rehmke is an unshackled woman writing unsanctioned words. This is precisely why you will love her work. Her poetry drips with the power that all women want: the liberty that lies outside the matrix, the force behind a mighty tornado, the protection of Medusa's head on Athena's shield. Her poems will leave you with an open mouth and an open heart. Few poets can deliver such potent images with so few words. Nicole is sure to have her name listed amongst the other legendary female poets: Angelou, Oliver, Diane, and Dickenson."
-Kimmery Moss, Author of *Wolf Mother*

"Nicole is a hurricane. She's so beautifully in touch with herself in a way most people aren't able to be. She can access so much and you can FEEL that in her poetry. Her words cut right into your soul. She makes you think and she makes you want to go light the world on fire and LIVE."
-Angie Brown, Singer and Songwriter

Cover art by Shelby McFadden of Maple Projects

Dedicated to my women.
We are cheering, laughing, yearning, feeling,
howling, and loving
in unison.

Eternal gratitude to Chelsie Diane, the best
poetry teacher in the world. Thank you for
helping me reclaim my one precious life as my
own.

SHE TASTES LIKE POSSIBILITY

A COLLECTION OF EMPOWERED POETRY

NICOLE PERRIELLA-REHMKE

Table of Contents

"And you, you scare people because you are whole all by yourself."
– Lauren Alex Hooper

Fire Devil

I feel flammable.
These smoldering embers
begging for your wind.
Intense heat rising.

Read it out loud.
Voice memo stirrings
for her ears.
Forceful exhalations.

How do the words sound
dancing with my lips?
Do they spark and sizzle?
A whirlwind induced by fire.

Did I dig deep enough
through the stiff mantle
to the yellow hot core?
Am I the spark or the ash?

She started a poem
with one of my lines.
A true poet compliment.
"Your fault," she laughs.

These women that understand me,
elevate my work with their words.
Your enthusiasm is like gas on my flame.
A fire swirl reaching forever higher.

My vocal cords vibrating
as I create a warm upward draft.
Swirling and pushing.
It all starts with a whirl of wind.

This fire devil can't be contained.
Let her consume all the things
and people that were hungry
for a fresh start anyway.
Charred.

Do Not Blush (After Virginia Woolf)

Applause
Cheering
My ancestors nudging me forward
to do what they could not.

Pink
Capri blue flame.
I pull a card
another
another.
Comfort in their wisdom.

Facing the truth
instead of drinking it away.
Here I sit
with my wine and Virginia Woolf.

A room of my own,
more than 500 a year.
Still interrupted
by a little girl that wants to be my twin.

Same striped dress,
dark underwear.
Joining me in the tub.
I will always let her in.

Purple iridescent nails,
dancing with my pen.
Blisters from rain boots rubbing,
nature walking back to myself.

The girl behind the counter
the teacher behind the desk
the woman
inside the mother.

She led me to that library
book sale,
no letter required.
I save a sacred seat for her.

She led the way
tasting our sentences
on her tongue,
assessing the mouth feel.

She tastes like possibility.
Chloe liked Olivia.
Do not start. Do not blush.
She's calling my poetry forward.

She Used to Sing on the Balcony

"You know what they say
about girls that add so much sugar
to their coffee?"
my Italian boss smirked.

Serving martinis in Spain.
A big NO made out of toothpicks.
My American heart
revealed to me.

Long white skirts
with no underwear.
Long blonde hair
with no responsibility.

I used to sing loud out on the balcony.
Wide open world inviting me to dance.
I twirled and laughed and jumped.

Learning Spanish by eavesdropping
at the cafe.
They're talking about tennis lessons.

Washing my clothes in the sink.
Hanging on the line.
Cockroach crunch under my boot.

The most alive
and free
and me.

Stick to Your Guns

"Is your brother dead yet?"
he said to me in the hallway.
My fourth grade heart
crumpled like a deflated parachute.

I remember when he got the call.
The mad rush to pack
that camo duffle bag.
Rucksack laundry, ironed just right.

Huddled with my mom,
recovering after that frantic goodbye.
"I'll never leave you, Mommy."
She smiled with a sigh.

She saved every letter
in a plastic photo album.
Gritty Gulf War sand
delivered from a world away.

Red Oldsmobile.
Turn it on and let it run.
A trip to nowhere.
82nd Airborne wings flying.

He made it back.
Took me to Fun Forest
and won me a little monkey toy,
maroon like his beret.

Little velcro hands
clinging to him with relief and pride.
Now my daughter plays with that monkey.
Long hugs and high fives.

Golf lessons with uncle.
She's not scared of losing him.
A wobbly fear now
etched into my DNA.

Talking on the phone every night.
The laugh, the sneeze,
so loud they make the baby cry.
Emotional infantry marching home.

He jumped out of that plane
and back into my life.
So grateful he stayed close.
Polkadots of love.

Be loud and be happy.
Just keep being here with me.
He made it home.
He made it safe.

Scratching at my Window

I can't sleep.
The poetry is scratching at my window.
Meow.
Let me in from the rain.

Tail curled around my leg
Purring sweet nothings
Teasing
with her affection.

I sneeze
and swell
congested with words
that must come out.

The dander
sprinkled invisibly
over every surface
like my poems.

Out of grasp
and right here
taking up all the space.
My voice changes.

I need to breathe.
Write them down.
Feel it all.
Jump out the window.

Discipline

Peeing my pants
in the air
held up by my shirt.
Wide feet on hardwood floor.
Big fist on my chest.
My thumbnail peeling up white paint.
Satisfying lines on the stairs.
Getting caught.
The danger.
Did I know that was going to happen?

Good

I was good when I wanted to make money.
I was good when I forgot about your birthday.
I was good when you saw those pictures.
I was good when you judged me.
I was good when you kicked me out.
I was good when you yelled at me
                and forgot who the fuck I am.
I was good when I got caught
                and cried when you took my picture.
I was good when they pulled me over.
I was good when I was ready to leave.
I was good when you fell off the swing.
I was good when I was rude.
I was good when I pushed all the limits.
I am good.

It's Mine

I was in charge all along.
I was waiting on you
and you were watching me.
I felt powerless
but you were tracking my movements.
You couldn't tell me directly
but the truth revealed itself.
Now I know
I set the tone.
I decide.
They stalk me and watch me
so I dress up
and give them a good show.
The first one's free.
Blow a kiss.
Claim the job,
the crown that was mine all along.

Call Me By My Rightful Name

Stacks of journals,
empty pages eagerly awaiting
my words.
Fill me up.

Tickle me with your pen.
Massage the leather.
Contented sigh
pulling truth from your marrow.

Sweeping out the atrium
with wave-like contractions.
A small collection chamber
alchemizing these sensations.

Cardiomyoctes injected
into uninjured hearts
demonstrates evidence
of cell to cell coupling.

The science and the spiritual
weave in and out.
What world do I want to live in?
Can one save me from the other?

Tell me a deeper truth
I can't find in your prescriptions.
Those bottles and diagnoses.
No side effects thank you please.

Finding a new OB/GYN
because I refuse to be labeled
high-risk.
I demand you call me by my rightful name.

"It might be pseudocyesis,"
she said to me.
No number of false negatives
can change what I believe.

Seat reclined, age seven
in my dad's pick-up truck.
He taught me how to command
my internal handymen.

The writing keeps me healthy.
It's the stuck feelings that scare me.
Resentment criteria.
Subcutaneous bacteria.

A Secure Man

It takes a secure man
to accept his woman
when she writes poetry about past lovers.

It takes a secure man
to love her quirks and peccadillos even when
they inconvenience him.

It takes a secure man
to apologize sincerely and
take responsibility for his actions.

It takes a secure man
to change her pad after surgery
and call it intimacy.

It takes a secure man
to dig out the lost diaphragm
like we live in the seventies.

It takes a secure man
to put his frustration aside and
parent from love and patience.

It takes a secure man
to hand finances over to his woman and
trust that she can handle business.

It takes a secure man.

Things I Love and Am Not Sorry For

I love it when you ask me if I'm trolling you.
I love it when you scratch my back
        and start rubbing.
I love it when you kiss my clavicle.
I love it when you cook for me.
        Blue cheese topping.
I love it when I hear you two laughing.
I love it when you help me get dressed
        for poetry class.
I love it when you offer your elbow.
I love it when you make gold crowns
        for date night at home.
I love it when you make 3D pop up cards.
        Middle finger and a man card.
I love knowing I get the best of you.
I love it when you roll your eyes
        but secretly like it.
I love it when you give me all your money.
I love it when you greet me on the porch.
I love it when you fix the running toilet.
I love it when you research everything.
I love it when you help my parents.
I love it when you lock the door.

Protected

Tired cheek on warm chest.
Her torso pressed against my back.
Contented sigh
wrapped in clean white sheets.

Dissolving into goo
liquifying any lesser love.
It streams out
and drips down red.

My insides melting.
Fluid breaking down
this antiquated caterpillar body
into undifferentiated imaginal cells.

In this safe haven home,
chrysalis transformation.
Visualizing how I want my insides
to rearrange me.

My opalescent wings
curled around us gently,
aligning in this sacred rest.
Preparing to expand.

Let me stay a little longer
curled in this cocoon of comfort,
protected from what I know
is coming for me.

Does It Fit?

Driving home from the airport
big hills, wide-leaved trees in
my little taxi.
The same conversation again and again.

I'm used to seeing boys with guns now.
At every doorway
every entrance
can't grow a full beard yet.

Dating a man is like
trying on a life.
Does this fit?
Can I see myself here?
Is this the life I want to choose forever?

There was a brief window
in my early 20's
when I would date a guy
just to try it.
No agenda.
Even better if they had a set end-point
built in.
"Oh he's going to Boot Camp."
"Oh he's moving to China."

Let me ride on your motorcycle.
Let me sing in your band.
Let me.

Teach me the Spanish of late night,
tired whispers,
first thing in the morning greetings.

Show me the song lyrics
that speak to your heart
make your body move.
Take me to your home in the campo
with the wood ceiling.
Swatting monster bugs with a tennis racket

I visit in my dreams
and it feels so familiar.
A home of mine that's not mine.

Briefly

Aguardiente in a little cup
hanging from a red string around my neck.
The crunch of chicharron,
side of avocado with everything.
I miss ajiaco.
That was my favorite.

You dream so big.
The world as your playground.
My hand fits in yours.
A smile that takes up your whole face.
Walking across the Brooklyn Bridge.
Juanes at Madison Square Garden.
What are the chances?

I could tell you were proud
to be with me.
That's a good feeling.
Your teary eyes next to my hospital bed
as I spoke to my parents a world away.

You took me to the hospital
and they admitted me
when my T-cell count was too low
fighting a stomach bacteria.

Running to the bathroom
when the antibiotics hit,
almost ripping out the IV.
Hell depleting me

You called me linda
Beautiful.
You read my journal
and we went to war.

I didn't take responsibility.
Mad about something else.
That's a pattern.
I see it now.

Forget who I kissed.
Forget where I was.
You both read my journal
and I got caught.

Why do I keep writing?
I can't not.
All the secrets
on the page.
They free me.

Jealousy

He's funny.
Bitch, don't tell me about my man.
Sidle up beside him
I would pee on him if I could.

He's funny.
Sit. Down.
Those jokes are for me.
That brain is mine.

He's funny.
His eyes are for watching me.
Piercing blue with straight lashes
Can you smell me on him?

He's funny.
That's my broad back to scratch.
Each mole mapping my land.
Marking my territory.

He's funny.
I watch you laugh
knowing his voice says my name.
He's on a roll. Over.

He's funny.
His rough hands on my curves.
Estrus cycle raising her rear
Doesn't it feel good to be owned by me?

He's funny.
His hair between my fingers.
Fetching my drink.
Heel.

Restraint

I curse you with lips sealed
bound by my own restraint.
It's your tone that scorches my back.
Our tinder ignites fast and easy.
Small dead limbs thinner than a pencil
under the live canopy of pine trees.
The words ablaze in my throat
ready to incinerate this whole fucking place.
Instead I swallow the burning
and unload the dishwasher.

Ode to my Shadow

I claw those words out
of your mouth.
Give them to me.
I crave your affirmations.
I take a bite and let the blood
drip
down my chin,
as I sigh with relief,
with reassurance.
Tell me more.
Give me more.
Fill me up with your words.
Your love.
Your admiration.
I love that shit.
I need it like food.
Fuel me with your words.
Pour them in.
Let them wash over me.
I'm a greedy bitch.
Send it in an email,
cute flower greeting cards,
dripping with the blood
my vampiress soul will lap up,
lick up
like ecstatic sustenance.
Give it to me.
Sweet nothings are everything.
Feed me.

Overflowing From Within

A tornado makes a roaring sound
like a fast-moving train.

This roar starts as a grumble,
a noticing
a hint.
Don't forget a can opener or a knife.

That rumble in the distance
The smell of wet concrete
My sky is cracking.
Bolts lighting up my eyes.

You say I complain
about problems I created.
You're right.
I expect the best.
I expect ease.
I complain about my old creations
until I change

them.

Are you scared
that I'm going to complain
first?
And then change
my relationship with you?

Batten down the hatches.
It's coming.
My storm is brewing.
Complaint siren signaling.
Marine-grade plywood
offers superior protection
against my gale.

Keep your valuables
in waterproof bins.
My flood waters rising
overflowing from within.

Raw Nose Tip

Raw nose tip from your stubble.
Peeling away my fake eyelashes.
Peeling away the shell of me.
Wanting someone to really see me,
know me.

You tell me about your ex-girlfriend,
the Ralph Lauren model,
the one you end up marrying.
I'm not even jealous.
I'm the one who knocked your Oxford oar
off the wall.

You and your Lamborghini
gave me the full Manhattan experience.

You asked me what kind of art I like.
I didn't know how to respond.
"Modern?"
That was the best question
you could have asked
to reveal the untouched places of my heart,
the poetry still locked inside.

Thank You For Understanding

It's just a poem.
I made it up.
It's all true.
What's it bringing up in you?

I'm Breaking Out of the Matrix

How can she howl at night
and greet my kids in the morning?
How can she dance naked under the moon
and speak sugary sweet at noon?

You don't own me.
Where in my contract
does it say I have to please you?
Dance nice girl, right on cue.

Where does it say to make everyone happy
all the time?
Where is that written?
Why is it written in my mind?
Why can't boundaries be kind?

I thought I had to wait
to publish this
until after I retired.
Could a poem get you fired?

A teacher can't do this.
She can't be this wild.
Wait 22 more years please.
Look up at me from your knees.

How can she be all this?
Refusing to get in the box
I make so much more money than you.
Could all these things be true?

Secret slithering sorceress
She's in me. She never left.
Feelings withheld, lips sealed.
Medusa's head on Athena's shield.

I Am What I Say I Am

These aren't your grandmother's words.
They are the incantation
she would have written
if she were freer.
If she hadn't married at 19.
If he hadn't burned them all.

These are the spells
she cast in her mind
that I get to say out loud,
scream out loud.
I am what I say I am.
I am everything.

She's So Hot

Boudoir photo shoot
Lined lids closed
Low back arch
Knees spread wide

Velvet vixen
turning up the volume
of her own self love.
Rolling in her beauty.

Reveal it all
Shed it all
Seeing herself as an object of desire
in the camera lens reflection.

She shudders with pleasure.
That smile started somewhere
deep within.
Rosy from all that oxygen.

Smoke show
Sultry smooth sensations.
Head held high
happily healing her heart.

What has she been eating?
Consuming those old fears,
alchemizing them into gold.
Shining riches right out through her skin.

Pop! Pop! Pop!
Dopamine fireworks inciting
her cerebral orgasm.
Her neuroplasticity is so hot.

You can't help but love her and her delulu.
Her lean towards happy.
Her laugh making me laugh.
Drunk on endorphins.

The water she consumes
lubricating infinite ideas
as they flow out
and spill out onto the page.

Oh did she splash you?
Her ink on your canvas.
Witness.
The shutter click flick.

A Woman Like Her

A woman like her doesn't stay for long
with language like that.
She's never stalled,
never stuck.

She can sense the change
of the wind,
the taste in the air,
something sour.

Women like her have
thick steel hulls
that can withstand
the ravages of a storm.

Her vessel might list
to one side
revealing her other.
She knows how to weather.

A woman like her
smooth sails toward clear sky,
the clean horizon.
The next adventure is calling.

Her future trips
filling her with love and hope.
When the sailors disembark,
she's on to the next voyage.

Forgiveness

I left.
Read the goodbye letter
voice calm on the phone
surprised me with that.
Somehow
I left the door open.

My Man

My man doesn't speckle toothpaste
on the mirror.
My man doesn't call for help.
He fucking figures it out.

Sweat soaks through his shirt
as he cleans my uncle's apartment
except for the patch on his chest,
shaped like a heart.

My man shaves off the rest of my dad's hair
after brain surgery.
The little tufts blow off the deck.
Both my hearts so tender outside me.

My man pushes on my hips
and breathes with me at prenatal yoga.
The tears in my eyes
as he stares into mine.

My man holds the line
when I want to comfort
and she needs a firm limit.
He's the strength for us all.

My man joins me in the tub
and I soak
in all his love
and attention.

My man's not going
to your black tie birthday party.
He's under the house thawing a pipe.
My man's not going out with the guys.
He's in the garage painting her a masterpiece.

My man notices the change in my voice
when the cats get in.
We leave and he stays close
buying me Claritin.

My man will be on time.
Early.
He has never once left me waiting, wondering.
His figure is as dependable as death.

My man filled this pen with fresh ink.
Gifts me leather journals with my initials.
He forgives me
when I read off my anger
and scorch us to the ground
again.

Sanctuary

Early morning quiet.
A clean page.
Raindrops sending me
encrypted messages
from me to me.

Your Face in My Mirror

When you apologized
it caught me by surprise
for not playing with me more.

Your index finger tracing
the hills of our backs,
drawing a patient picture.

Coffee sips in floral mugs,
flipping newspaper pages.
You save the Sudoku for me.

Generous pours
and contented smiles.
Love tokens every visit.

I see myself as a link
in a very long chain
of incredible women.
Witches.

Track the scent, names always changing.
Burnt on the stake;
she's so amazing.

You woke when she died.
You felt it. You knew.
The veil is thin, and I'm reaching through.

Studying for the CPA exam,
flashcards with Kay.
Accounting for what's been missing.

Potions in the kitchen, love through food
until it's too much.
What are we stuffing?

Drown in a river
Drown in a goblet
The feelings we suppress.

A full education with no expectation.
Just don't embarrass your husband
at cocktail parties.

Smoking cigarettes
in the garage,
happily exiled with your book.

You showed me the commitment
required to provide.
Daycare at 6 weeks.

Paid to connect.
We draw out the stories
and spin them into magic.

You have a reason to decorate now.
I gave you that
and your heart keeps pouring.

Shedding preemptive tears.
A grief waiting for me someday.
I shake it away and say,
"That jacket looks really good on you,
Mom."

Serve Me

I am the Queen of this house.
As I stir the lentil soup
my love blessing
this potion.
Every hug, every look
calm and regal
that long sensual breath
of peaceful knowing.
Reading my book after dinner
on my pink throne,
surrounded by beauty.
My energy is potent here.
Marinating in this feeling,
soaking up the juice.
Serve me.

Wishes Fulfilled

I'm always by the water.
Creaking swings and cold grey blue
peace and solitude.

I see her by the water.
Rocky beach, flat horizon
waves singing her to sleep.

She feels herself by the water.
He makes the coffee breakfast.
She goes upstairs to write.

She's inspired by the water.
Electric car to the little shop
connected to the island.

So much friendship by the water.
Dusky picnics, watermelon dripping.
Your mom brought her love to the water.

Looking out by the water
her office desk by the window.
Royalties make this view.

Her delusion by the water.
The reality she created.
Imagination swells first.

They can't see her by the water
blending with the mist.
Diadem hidden in wavy hair.

Giggles in the Morning

You two are off
on a secret mission
buying donuts at the store.

Every time I pretend to be surprised.
Your jack-o'-lantern smile handing me rainbow
carnations.

Homemade Halloween decorations
taped to all the doors.
I love you mama.
Sweet dreams.

The curl of your hair
The blue eyes he gave you
The eyes I fell in love with
shine back at me twice.

I can finally sit on a chair
at the pool
and watch you swim.
I wondered if this day would ever come.

My only child
We get one round of this.
I remind myself to pay attention.
Cherish the love notes she writes me.

Thank you for bringing back the magic.
The fairies and mystery and love.
"I see them
because I believe."

This is the life I dreamed of.
My strong, reliable husband.
My sweet, sweet daughter
making this home holy,
sacred,
ours.

Angel's Envy

For my women
hidden behind a wall of books.
Angel's Envy on ice.
Naughty sequins winking.

My support system sipping
on speakeasy sophistication.
Custom cocktails
in clear crystal goblets.

The most gorgeous hotel
founded by women,
for my founding women.
This is the Founders Club.

Those late night conversations,
closed door confessions.
Allowing myself to be seen,
to be fully known.

She brought the candles
and laughed as she sang.
Layers of my life overlapping.
You are the frosting.

Men pouring drinks.
Sculpted mustaches
serving divine feminine.
Stirred and shaken.

Serene spirits sparkling
in this secluded scene.
Forever enriched by the deep love
of my sisters.

About the Author

Nicole Perriella-Rehmke is an award-winning educator, author and poet who lives in Snoqualmie, Washington, with her husband and daughter. She tells empowering stories in her life, in her classroom and on her podcast, *Manifesting Book Magic*. Her children's book, *Except for All That Noise*, won the Golden Wizard Book Prize and celebrates sensory differences. This is her first book of poetry.
@manifestingbookmagic